North Derbyshire Collieries

on old picture postcards

Alan Bower

1. Alfreton Colliery (1886-1968) was one of Blackwell Colliery Co's mines and at the time of closure employed 652 men. The engine shed and another small building remain in the middle of the industrial estate. Several private company wagons can be seen in the foreground belonging to coal merchants in the London area, along with the colliery's own, and those of the London, Midland and Scottish Railway. Postcard published by Glover of Alfreton and Kirkby.

GW00659201

£3.50

INTRODUCTION

Coalmining has been carried on in Derbyshire for centuries. Records show that coal was being mined at Morley and Smalley in the 13th century, Stretton and Wingerworth in the 14th, Codnor a century later, and Tibshelf in the 16th century. In the 1300s, coal from the Alfreton area was supplied to the monks at Beauchief Abbey. These early mines would have been bell pits, working in relatively thick seams of coal near the surface. Evidence of pits like these have been found around the county.

The present coal mining industry owes its origins two centuries ago to the momentum of the Industrial Revolution. Coal production was closely linked with the iron industry, and the introduction of the steam engine and later growth of railways stimulated a huge demand for coal. In the 18th century there were some 25 pits in Derbyshire using Newcomen steam engines, in particular for pumping out water. As pits went deeper to meet the need for more coal they came across more water, a problem that has always beset the miner in Derbyshire.

The iron and coal industries grew up side by side in north-east Derbyshire, with some firms specialising in mining equipment. Transport was made easier firstly by canals and then railways, and production of both coal and iron in the county increased fourfold between 1841 and 1901. Iron companies such as Staveley, Clay Cross, Stanton and Butterley were among the largest colliery owners in the Midlands. Many collieries also had their own brickworks: nearby housing for the large workforce led to large concentrations of brickbuilt houses which often swallowed up the original settlements. The coal industry was to change the face of the landscape with its housing, its works and its waste tips.

Before the mid-19th century, boys as young as five were employed in the pits driving ponies and hauling baskets of coal. Females were not employed in the mines – unlike some parts of Britain. The Mines Act of 1872 prohibited the employment of very young children and led to improvements in conditions and safety.

The majority of seams in the area dipped or ran eastwards into Nottinghamshire. Silkstone seams produced good quality coal for household use, as well as gas and coke, while the Top Hard produced top grade coking coal for iron furnaces. The discovery of good coking coal at Clay Cross by George Stephenson induced him to buy as much land as he could and start his own Coal and Iron Co. It soon became known as the Clay Cross Co. and was the first to transport coal to London by rail. In 1908 the company won a gold medal for its coal at the Franco-British Exhibition in London. To celebrate this, and to advertise their prize-winning coal, they produced a set of 25 postcards showing their miners at work. The cards obviously aimed to show the best aspects of the industry, but remain as a valuable record of mining at the start of the 20th century. They were given away free with each payment for a coal delivery, and a full set could be redeemed for prizes like a canteen of cutlery.

The past fifty years have seen a steady reduction in the number of working pits in the area, and it is sobering to think that in 1906 there were 176 pits in the whole of Derbyshire, employing 52,000 people (of whom 41,000 worked underground) producing $16\frac{1}{4}$ million tons of coal.

Picture postcards were the most convenient and popular way of sending news and messages to friends and family in the 1902-14 period, and a craze grew up for collecting them. The publishers of postcards provided a huge variety of pictures for the public to buy, and these images now provide a valuable source material. Many of the cards included in this book were published by anonymous local photographers, but a few are the work of some of the biggest postcard firms in the area, for example Nadin and Waterhouse of Chesterfield. Dates and publishers of the cards are included in the captions where known.

Alan Bower
March 1993

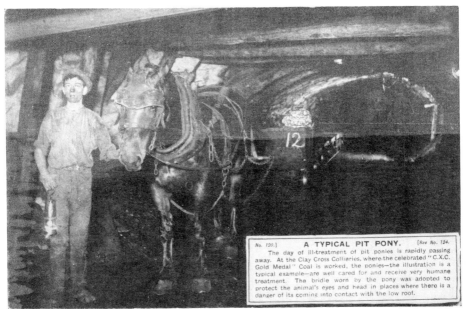

No. 120.] **A TYPICAL PIT PONY.** [See No. 124.

The day of ill-treatment of pit ponies is rapidly passing away. At the Clay Cross Collieries, where the celebrated "C.X.C. Gold Medal" Coal is worked, the ponies—the illustration is a typical example—are well cared for and receive very humane treatment. The bridle worn by the pony was adopted to protect the animal's eyes and head in places where there is a danger of its coming into contact with the low roof.

2. The Clay Cross Co. published a series of 25 postcards (numbered 100-124) featuring mining scenes. This card (no.120) forecasts the ending of ill-treatment of pit ponies, which suffered terrible back injuries in the pits.

Designed and published by Reflections of a Bygone Age,
Keyworth, Nottingham 1993
Reprinted 1994, 1995, 1998
and 2001

ISBN 0 946245 78 9

Printed by
Adlard Print and Typesetting Services,
Ruddington, Notts.

Front cover: Creswell Colliery, only recently closed, on a fine photographic card published by J. Binge at Creswell Post Office and sent to Fountain Dale near Mansfield in April 1914. To the left of the picture are huge piles of pit props, and on the right two men have positioned a wagon on the weighbridge for weighing.

Back cover (top): a team of "getters", one digging the coal out of the seam as his mate secures the roof with a pit prop. A shovel lies in the foreground for loading coal into the tubs. In many pits these were banned, and forks were used which allowed the smaller unwanted bits to fall through. Clay Cross series card no. 102.

(bottom): Shirland Colliery (1864-1965), owned by the Blackwell Colliery Co. There appears to be an unusual assortment of wooden buildings here, and a strange headgear which probably powered the screens. The railway to the colliery came up through a long tunnel from the next valley. There is nothing to recognise here now, as the site is a golf course.

Reverse text on one of the Clay Cross postcards, picture sides of which are featured throughout this book.

Acknowledgements: Chris Goodlad, for the loan of illus. 5; Cliff Williams, for the details on the Clay Cross Co. postcards; Eric Williamson (NCB Records, Bolsover), to whom I am indebted for helping with the relevant dates of colliery openings and closures.

4. Miners travelling on the Paddy train at the end of their shift. The man in the foreground is holding a pair of rubber gloves, suggesting he is an electrician. Clay Cross Co. card no.117.

3. Blackwell Colliery (1872-1969), known as "A" winning. After closure, the site was cleared apart from one building which remained as a stores and cable works. This colliery company even had its own hospital. The card, by an anonymous publisher, was posted to Grange-over-Sands in May 1905 with the message *"Perhaps you have never seen a colliery. If not you will not understand the various objects in this photo, but I will explain them when I see you. That colliery is about ¼ of a mile from our house."*

No. 117.]   [*See Nos. 115 & 122.*
THE COLLIERS' "MAIL!"
A RIDE IN THE DEPTHS.
Getters of the "C.X.C. Gold Medal" Coal returning
from the workings to the shaft after their day's work.

5. Barlborough Colliery (no.1 1873, no.2 1896-1928), situated on Boughton Lane at the north-eastern end of Clowne village. A few of the colliery houses still remain, though the site was cleared in the 1950s.

6. A rare view inside the blacksmith's shop at **Barlborough** on a card posted at Clowne in 1905. All manner of things for use around the colliery could be repaired or even made here.

Sheards Colliery
Dronfield,

7. Gosforth Pit, Sheards Colliery, Dronfield. This was a very small-scale pit, apparently opening around 1887 and closing early this century. The site on the edge of the hill is now a housing estate.

No. 111.]   [See No. 102.
"FOR MEN MUST WORK."
Getting and loading up the celebrated "C.X.C.
Gold Medal" Coal in one of the Clay Cross Co.'s Pits,
300 yards below ground.

8. "Getting" and "loading" coal from a narrow seam featured on Clay Cross card no.111. The men's number is chalked on the tub, for they were paid by the tub load.

9. Cotes Park (1850-1963) on a postcard published about 1906, showing the aftermath of a disaster. Sparks from a passing engine had set fire to the roof of the winding house which collapsed before being brought under control. This would have seriously delayed work at the colliery until it could be put back to use. The site is now an industrial estate, with Thornton's chocolate factory here.

No. 103.] **MAKING THE ROOF SAFE.** *[See No. 108.*
Colliers engaged in maintaining the safety of the roads, 300 yards below ground, along which the renowned "C.X.C. Gold Medal" Coal is conveyed from the workings to the shaft.

10. Three men are shearing up the roadway to make the roof safe and prevent it falling in. Clay Cross card no.103.

11. Clay Cross Company's no.2 pit, sunk in 1850 and situated in their iron works. A group of wagons can be seen under the screens being filled with coal, while a shunting engine waits at the side. The company published this card and preprinted the reverse for their own correspondence purposes.

No. 119.] GOING UP. [See No. 111.
"Tubs" of the celebrated "C.X.C. Gold Medal".
Coal arriving at the Pit bottom ready for hauling up
the shaft to the surface.

12. Full tubs of "C.X.C. Gold Medal" coal are being loaded into the cage for hauling up the shaft to the surface. The empties were taken out at the other side and brought around. No.119 in the long Clay Cross series.

13. Grassmoor Colliery (1875-1950), a large operation with five shafts. The main line of the Great Central Railway can be seen running through the middle of the colliery. The site is now a country park, with no sign of the pit remaining. Card posted at Chesterfield in August 1913.

No. 113.]　　　　**OFF UP.**　　　[See No. 122.
Colliers—getters of the "C.X.C. Gold Medal" Coal—being hauled from bottom of shaft to surface 300 yards above.

14. Miners at the end of their shift on their way back up to the surface. This was the easy part: they had probably had a long walk from their place of work to get here. Clay Cross card no.113.

15. Hartington Colliery (1879-1930). It is now hard to see where this colliery stood, but the houses at the far right of the colliery still stand on the road from Staveley to Renishaw.

No. 104.]   [See Nos. 116 & 119.
EN ROUTE FOR LONDON!
"C.X.C. Gold Medal" Coal in the first stage of its journey—300 yards from the surface—to the London consumer.

16. En route for London: a pit pony with a train of at least eight tubs of coal taking them to the shaft for hauling up to the surface. The pony is wearing a protective headgear, supposed to have been invented locally. No.104 in the 'Clay Cross' series.

Hardwick Colliery, Chesterfield.

17. Hardwick Colliery, Holmewood (1870-1968), quite a large colliery with its own coking ovens. The site is now an industrial estate covered by various factories. Card published by Alfred Rippon of Chesterfield.

No. 123.]   **A RESPONSIBLE WORK.**   [See No. 103.
To ensure the general safety of the Mine constant examinations are necessary. Here we see the inspection of the roof and machinery. The track is one of numerous ones along which the "C.X.C. Gold Medal" Coal is conveyed.

18. Safety checks are being made by what appears to be two deputies, judging by their sticks. One is inspecting the roof while the other is checking the cable for hauling the tubs on this quite sharp bend. Clay Cross card no.123.

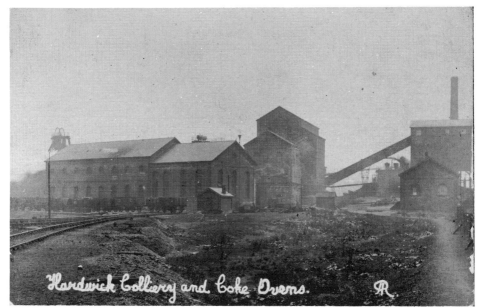

19. Another postcard view by Rippon showing the coke plant at **Hardwick Colliery.** The wagons on the left belong to different railway companies: Midland, London & North Western, and the Great Central, on whose line the pit was situated.

No. 107.] DOWN A COAL MINE.
Blacksmith performing his daily duties in the stables in one of the Pits producing the renowned "C.X.C. Gold Medal" Coal.

20. A blacksmith at work in an underground stable. Conditions varied from pit to pit for the ponies. While some were bad, others were looked after better than their counterparts on the surface. No.107 in the 'Clay Cross' series.

Clay Cross Company's N⁰. 5. & N⁰. 6. Coal Pits at Morton.

21. Nos. 5 & 6 at **Morton Colliery** (1863-1965), owned by the Clay Cross Co. The winding engine here pioneered Howes link motion and is still awaiting restoration. The screens are in the centre of the picture. Many of these buildings underwent changes, especially new headstocks, and although the colliery closed nearly thirty years ago, most of it still remains. Card published by the company itself.

22. Morton Colliery in the 1930s. The chimney and the buildings on the right have long since gone, but some of the buildings in the centre of the picture still survive.

23. Rare postcard of a wagon smash at **Morton Colliery**, sometime around 1910. A number of wagons had run out of the pit yard (as often happened!) and onto the main line. The steam crane, on the colliery line, is lifting damaged wagons. The signals in centre background are on the beginning of a branch line to Pilsley Colliery.

24. Pleasley Colliery (1883-1983), part of the Stanton Iron Works Co. For several years after closure, one of the headgear and winding house mechanisms was left standing. The colliery was one of the first to have underground electric lighting. This card was postally used from a village in Northamptonshire in August 1922.

MANNER'S COLLIERY.   ILKESTON.

25. Manners Colliery, Ilkeston (1877-1949) on a 'Peveril' series postcard. Few traces can be found of this once proud pit.

No. 118.]   [See No. 122.

THE WINDING ENGINE DRIVER.

These men hold the lives of hundreds of miners in their hands every day, and haul to the surface thousands of tons of the celebrated "C.X.C. Gold Medal" Coal.

26. The winding engine driver's job was a very skilled one and in many instances carried on by members of the same family. Morton's engine had a brass plate on one of the pistons bearing the names of the winders since 1865 (all called Wheeler). The winding house was kept in immaculate condition with all its gleaming brass work. 'Clay Cross' series no.118.

27. A fine shot of two shafts at **Shirebrook Colliery**, started in 1896, along with the screens and company wagons. The headgear was modernised in the 1960s and buildings have undergone changes but the layout remains much the same.

28. Shirebrook Colliery. A few of these buildings still remain, but the headstocks, made of wood, have long since been replaced.

29. Oxcroft Colliery, Shuttlewood Common. A superb
full of rubbish. There is nothing left of this site, which in
publisher, but the photo dates from c.1908. The colliery
pitch, tennis courts, bowling green and pavilion.

of a typical small pit with a line of tubs which appear to be
years has been opencasted. No indication of the postcard
s situated next to the pit and had a cricket ground, football

30. Tibshelf nos.3 & 4 pits on a 'Peveril' series card from 1905. The colliery, owned by the Babbington Coal Co., was open from 1870-1939. The card shows the extent of the buildings, including an engine shed in the centre with some shearlegs, supposedly to carry out engine repairs. Nothing is left of the colliery now; the site is an industrial estate.

No. 124. **ARRIVAL AT DAYLIGHT.** [*See No. 120.*]
Pony arriving at the top of the shaft after nearly 20 years in the bowels of the earth. Ponies not infrequently spend nearly the whole of their lives underground. This photo was taken at one of the Clay Cross Mines where the celebrated "C.X.C. Gold Medal" Coal is produced.

31. Arrival above ground at daylight, **Parkhouse Colliery** (1866-1962). A pit pony has been brought to the surface, apparently to retirement after spending 20 years underground. On the left of the picture are the screens. The gentleman on the right, wearing slippers and a smoking cap (!!), is Gaffer Dunn. Clay Cross card no.124.

This pony took part in the procession today (July 2nd) in aid of the Hospital.

"BILLY," Gang Pony at the South Normanton Colliery.

32. Billy the Gang Pony at **South Normanton Colliery.** Billy, we are told on the reverse of the card, had given 24 years service without a day off, working at the bottom of the shaft. He worked faithfully all day until the six knocks, marking the end of his shift, told him to return to his stable. Billy was 26 years old at the time. The writer of the card, sent to an address in Sandal, Yorkshire, in July 1910, says: *"this pony took part in the procession today (July 2nd) in aid of the Hospital."*

No. 106.]   **PAY-DAY.**
Coal-getters entering Pay Office for their wages after a week's work getting the "C.X.C. Gold Medai" Coal. The weekly pay-bill totals some £5,000.

33. Pay-day, Clay Cross series card no.106. A group of men line up at the time office, situated in the iron works of the company's no.2 pit. Moulds for castings can be seen stacked in the background. The weekly wage bill, according to the text on the card, totalled £5,000.

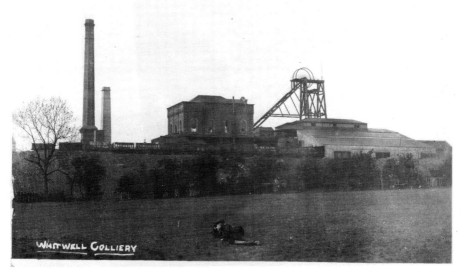

34. Whitwell Colliery (1890-1986), owned by the Shireoaks Colliery Co. Some of the company's wagons can be seen here coming out of the screens along with one belonging to Beaumonts of Ipswich. The card was posted to Leicester in August 1913.

35. Beighton Colliery and coke ovens. One or two of the larger collieries had their own coking ovens, often for supplying local iron works. The photographic card here shows an enormous coal bunker, probably of around 500 tons capacity, being fed by an aerial ropeway from the nearby colliery, the headstocks of which can just be seen.

36. Published locally by the London Stores, this card features **Langwith Colliery** (1878-1979), belonging to the Shirebrook Coal & Iron Co. Water was always a problem here, and pumping carried on for several years after its closure to relieve flooding at Cresswell. The site was cleared and nothing now remains. Card posted to Portsmouth in August 1936: *"Today I have been to Duke of Portland's Estate, Welbeck Abbey. He is the owner of all the land and collieries around."*

37. North Midlands Coal owners Rescue Station on Infirmary Road, Chesterfield. The postcard was published in 1919, shortly after the station was opened. The fire engine, ambulance and crew can be seen left of centre. The houses – far above the standard of miners' houses at the time – were built for the crews.

Please write for prices for House Coal, Cast Iron, Iron Pipes, Lime, Pig Iron, Fuel Economiser, &c., &c.

CLAY CROSS COMPANY. VIEW SHOWING Nº9 & Nº11 COAL PITS.

38. Avenue Colliery, the Clay Cross Co's nos. 9 & 11 pits, begun in 1881 and 1857 respectively. These two shafts were a fair way apart, as can be seen from the chimney in the background, and were situated near Clay Cross station. The company issued the postcard, and added an overprint advertising their goods.

FORDS COLLIERY Nº1 RESCUE TEAM

39. Fords Colliery no.1 rescue team at Marehay Main Collieries, Ripley. This photograph – and many others of similar teams – was taken at Chesterfield Mines Rescue Station *(see illus. 37),* probably after some training session. The men have their breathing apparatus and electric lights. Did the dog go down with them?

40. Southgate Colliery (1875-1929), Clowne. This was abandoned in 1929 after an inrush of water from the abandoned Oxcroft pit. In 1955, it was re-opened to make a connection with the Creswell High Hazel seams, but this was never completed and in 1961 the shafts were filled and capped, and the site cleared. Postcard sent from Clowne on 24th December 1907 as a Christmas/New Year greeting.

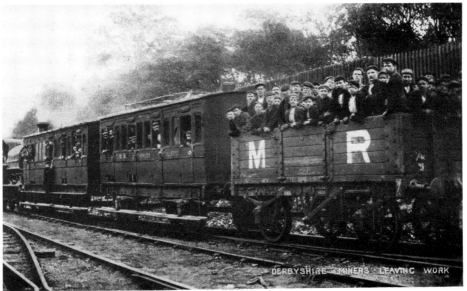

41. Miners leaving work (in style) on a postcard published in the 'Peveril' series and posted at Ilkeston in March 1907. The old third-class carriage has 'Shipley Colliery Co.' on the outside.

42. Bolsover Colliery Club, New Bolsover Model Village, built in 1904 by the colliery for their workpeople and families. 'Cutts' series postcard, sent from Carr Vale in October 1916.

No. 114.]   *[See Nos. 109 & 110.*
COLLIERS IN CAMP.
Getters of the "C.X.C. Gold Medal" Coal undergoing their fortnight's Territorial training in the Peak of Derbyshire.

43. Once a year some miners were lucky to escape work for a fortnight to go to camp and train as members of the Territorials. This scene, on 'Clay Cross' series card no.114, is in the Peak District.

44. Alfreton Colliery, with some of the pit ponies and drivers during Wakes Week, when they were let out to take part in races. Not all the colliery owners allowed this, and many pit ponies never left underground till it was time for the knacker's yard. The building in the centre still remained in recent years. Card published by G.S. Ellis of Albert Street, Mansfield, about 1920.

45. Coal picking on the spoil heaps of **Brockwell Colliery,** Chesterfield, during the strike of 1912. All the small coal was usually tipped away as unsuitable, and could be retrieved in times of crisis: with their supply of fuel cut off, families turned to the tips to hunt for coal.

Coal Pickers, Ilkeston—Strike, 1912.

46. Bestwick's series postcard, sent from Ilkeston in July 1915, showing coal-picking on the spoil heaps at **Manners Colliery,** Ilkeston, during the 1912 strike. This lasted for six weeks and was successful in securing a legally-guaranteed minimum wage for the miners, albeit not as high as they wanted.

47. Derbyshire Miners Union Headquarters, Saltergate, Chesterfield. This postcard, by J.H. Waterhouse, shows the unveiling of statues of Mr. Haslam and Mr. W.E. Harvey, local M.P.s and founders of the union, on 26th June 1915.

48. A postcard by C.H. Nadin of West Bars, Chesterfield, featuring a miners' demonstration in August 1907 in Market Square, Chesterfield. This was an annual holiday for miners and their families: they processed through the town with their colourful union banners, starting at Saltergate football ground and ending up in the Market Place. After this, they went off to Queens Park for a picnic.

49. Blackwell Colliery Football Club, 1910. Miners worked long hours and the little spare time they had was usually taken up with some activity. Most collieries supported an Institute or Miners' Welfare. Blackwell had football, cricket and bowls teams.

50. Creswell Colliery had their cricket pitch next to the pit itself. I was scorer for Morton Colliery Cricket Club in my teens and will always remember tales from the old-timers who said they had hit a ball so high it had dropped down the pit chimney and knocked out the stoker! Postcard by Harding.

51. Creswell Colliery Band in 1926, showing off two trophies they won at Belle Vue (one of the brass band circuit's most prestigious awards) and Newcastle in the previous year.

52. Swanwick Colliery Silver Prize Band. There were few pits without a brass band. Swanwick are pictured here outside Alfreton Miners Welfare about 1928.

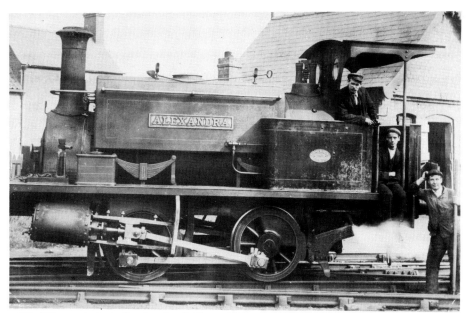

53. "Alexandra" at Southgate Colliery, Clowne. This engine was built by Manning Wardell & Co. of Leeds in 1902. Sad to say, the vast majority of these proud little engines are no longer with us. I remember many a colliery engine back in the 1960s being scrapped when diesel engines replaced them or the pit was closing.

54. Derbyshire Miners' Convalescent Home at Skegness, built at a cost of £110,000 and opened in 1928 by Lord Chelmsford. This card was published by C. & A.G. Lewis and posted from the seaside resort to an address in Shirland in August 1928.

No. 122.]   [See Nos. 113 & 118.

ARRIVING AT THE SURFACE.

Cage with Clay Cross Colliers arriving at the top of the
shaft after a day's work in one of the Pits producing the
"C.X.C. Gold Medal" Coal.

55. 'Clay Cross' series card no.122, showing miners arriving at a shaft top after a day's work.

56. Smokey Joe, a chimney sweep who worked in the Alfreton area.

No. 116.]   [See No. 104.

ARRIVAL OF COAL AT PIT SHAFT.

"C.X.C. Gold Medal" Coal arriving at the bottom
of the shaft ready for hauling to the surface 300
yards above.

57. Clay Cross card no.116. Full tubs waiting to go up the shaft with a pit pony about to take the empties back to the coalface.

No. 105.]   **ON THE BELT.**

One of the travelling tables (belts) along which the
"C.X.C. Gold Medal" Coal is passed during its preparation
for the London Market.

58. Coal was screened on the belt, with rock and rubbish thrown out and the coal graded into sizes. It was a backbreaking job, usually given to the old or those who had been injured, and it was one of the lowest-paid. Clay Cross card no.105.